VIA Folios 130

The Sonnetarium

The Sonnetarium

Lewis Turco

BORDIGHERA PRESS

Library of Congress Control Number: 2017917373

Printed in the United States.

Published by
BORDIGHERA PRESS
John D. Calandra Italian American Institute
25 West 43rd Street, 17th Floor
New York, NY 10036

VIA FOLIOS 130
ISBN 978-1-59954-126-6

Contents

9   Foreword
        The Foreword Blues

13   Sleeping with Love
        Sleeping with Love
        Gaea's Welcome
        Smallage
        Younger in Our Dreams
        Nocturne
        Embrace
        Body Part

21   Serenade
        Amoreuse
        The West Chester Carol
        Leola
        Selene
        Sports Sexual Harassment Embarrassment
        Currency
        Venus' Arbor
        Sonnets of Gold

33   Seasoning
        Seasoning
        A Letter from London
        Thanksgiving Sonnet
        Winter Blinds
        Cursory Comment
        The Xmas Blues
        Tyranny
        The Mild Winter Blues
        Winter Panes
        Yearsend

45   Simulacra
        Shall I Compare Thee to a Winter's Day?
        Simulacrum Sonnet

The Oil Spill Blues
Lisbon
Girlguy
The Blues Blues
Catachresis
The Wormy Blues
The Wannabe Blues
The Blue Flag
Assumptions

59   Prufrock's Dream
Dreaming Stories
The Born-Again Blueth
The Oxymoronic Blues
The Department Meeting Blues
When Did I Love Thee?
Epistle in Depression
Prufrock's Dream
Prufrock in a Nutshell
Bloomsday
A Midsummer Night's Partsong

71   The Unremembered
The Journey
The Barn Owl
Knell for John Knell
Hello and Goodbye
Elegiac Sonnet
The Unremembered
Cosmology

81   CORONATIONS
The Crown of Blues
A Crown for Don
Cousin Josephine
An Old Poet's Reply

Foreword

THE FOREWORD BLUES

Wesli Court said I should write a book,
A bunch of blues—enough to fill a book,
And he'd design the cover. I said, "Look,

If you'll write half of them, then I will choose
A ball-point pen, a felt-tip—I will choose
To join you in a modicum of blues."

And that's the reason, Reader, we are here—
You, Wes and me—we three assembled here
Among these turning leaves yellow and sere.

We hope you'll think the words we write are fine,
Our writing bold and dark, but our wordage fine . . . ,
At least we hope you'll like the cover design.

Envoy Epilogue

Go, little book of sorrows, cares and woes,
But Wesli's gone. Where? Only goodness knows.

Sleeping with Love

SLEEPING WITH LOVE

Death comes to sleep with Love when one is born,
Yes, Death must bed with Love when we are born:
The hope of Love forever is forlorn.

The dream of Love eternally is torn
Asunder. Love eternally is torn
From under us. Our winding sheets are worn

From birth until that day when Love must mourn
The life that came to pass—then Love will mourn
The hope of life eternally forlorn.

The night will fill with the notes of the final horn,
Moonlight illuminates the sounding horn—
We will find why our winding sheets were worn.

Yes, Death must sleep with Love when we are born;
We will find why our winding sheets were worn.

GAEA'S WELCOME

The opening of my womb is here to win.
If you are chary you may deem it sin
To enter out of wedlock—not so nature
Which has no use for anything that's "pure,"
Only for usages that ensure survival
Of the species, like the strongest rival
Prevailing over weaker suitors so
That the hardiest genes manage to go
Forward into time and reproduce
The hardier. This is the only ruse
Used by the universe to render death
Incapable of conquering my breath.

So come all you who fear to fade and fail!
You shall be used again. Do not bewail.

SMALLAGE

The serpent was a liar. Eve swallowed it,
Core and all, every jot and tittle.
Basically we've learned a tiny bit,

But not a lot, about Creation. Little
Did we understand the more we knew,
The more we found we'd just begun to whittle

Away at what there is. We found a few
New laws, and then discovered there are others
Lying low beneath them. What seemed true

Turned out to be but half-truths and Cain's mother's
Knowledge did not obviate school, college,
Or hard knocks for his sisters or his brothers

Down the line. It behooves us to acknowledge
We'll never know immensities, just smallage.

NOCTURNE

On pleated wings the sleepless mind descends
The stair of dream, its coils encircling sounds
That seep through windowpanes. The rabid hounds
Of midnight bay along the trail of winds.
The reptile brain creeps through forbidden fens
Of solitary thought. There are no bounds
To these morasses, these oppressive grounds.
As dread advances solitude impends.

But morning tints the windowpane at last;
The mind gives up to fantasy's dim hordes.
The moat of night has finally been passed.
Oblivion takes umbrage at the swords
Of intellect and dulls them in the vast
Abyss of entity which sleep affords.

EMBRACE

The winter is wearing its whitest winter face.
The wind is seeping under the windowsill
And sifting along the floor to where we fill
Silence with dreams of spring. We would erase
This season of frozen starlight without a trace
If we knew how. Behind our home the mill
Has felled itself: its stones ignore the still
Waters of the stream; once, they would race
Against the turning wheel, their currents lace
Figures of froth in its channel down the hill.
Now it has beards of rime that are grim and chill
And mimic the cumuli of inner space.

May those clouds burst to let the brook fulfill
Its destiny to destroy starlight's embrace!

BODY PART

I offer you the same old gift again:
This ancient shriveled organ of my flesh
That we have used since who remembers when?

It's shoddy now, but it was strong and fresh
When we were young. You held it in your hand
And felt its pulse when we had seed to thresh.

 It throbbed for you and needed no command
To flame and ache when it was called upon
To do its duty, dilate and expand

To fill the evening or the breaking dawn,
The morn or afternoon with the lover's art . . . ,
So many years have passed now and have gone

To seed, so many organs have come apart—
Still, I offer you this same old heart.

Serenade

AMOREUSE

These words are all of me that I may show
To name you what I am. For what I am
Is words, and what you are is merely an
Idea wrapped in syllables. I'll know

You when I name you "body" and you tremble
"love" in warm return. The shape, the form
Is blank if naming's not the portrait's frame.
The flame must be ignited with a symbol.

I'll quote you yesterdays if you will speak
Tomorrows made from each of our todays,
The names of love stacked in a cairn of sighs
In the name of Eros and for his namesake.

Seek movement with me, for, though actions shout
I've merely words to tell what we're about.

THE WEST CHESTER CAROL
Exploring Form & Narrative

Erato and her sisters took a spin,
A ride on Zephyr . . . just a little spin
To West Chester, PA, where they dropped in

To say "Hello" to all their kith and kin,
Their cousins and their friends, both kith and kin.
Polyhymnia said, "There is no sin

Attached to such a visit—we'll merely chin
A bit, just talk some shop; we'll simply chin
About poetic form and the ears of tin

Some minstrels have who make an awful din
When they strike up the band: an awful din
Instead of music, much to my chagrin."

Calliope just snorted. "I want to win
The Marathon, not wrestle for a pin."

LEOLA

It goes away, Leola, as the rabble
Hooves have done. The prairies linger. None,
No, none may know the stallion with his sable
Mane for long, nor his desire. Gone

Are the souls of brontosaurs, for they have run
Their feather course, for all I know, Leola.
This is true, though: oceans dwell as one
Among the continents. Look through a hollow

Rush, Leola: sight is vaguely dry
And limited, although the hint of light
Arrows down the reed to meet the eye,
To pierce the iris in its yolk of white.

Put down the hollow reed now. Let it be.
Peer through your flesh or mine. What do you see?

SELENE

You've lost at the game of love, Endymion,
And so have I. The forfeiture is steep
For those who would contend. Selene has won.
One seldom wins at last, for it is sleep

That triumphs after all. There is your vale,
Endymion: you slumber while the hounds
Hunt their quarry. Your mistress will prevail
At masques and balls. She makes her evening rounds

While you pursue your dreams. She knows that sport
Is in the sap and blood of spring, not shadow.
Selene will choose the quick for her consort,
The play of moonlight in a summer meadow.

Will you dream on, Endymion, to rue
The pulsing game your mistress offers you?

SPORTS SEXUAL HARASSMENT EMBARRASSMENT 2010
After losing to Baltimore the Jets lose again

The day when Ines Sainz came marching in
To tackle the Jets' steamy locker room
And get an interview on her recorder
She billed herself "the hottest sports reporter
In Mexico." The players were abloom,
Sweaty and florid, showing a lot of skin.
She tried hard not to notice they had shed
Their shorts and towels—at least that's what she said.

But it was hard to miss each whistle, call,
And all the balls the coaches threw to land
Not far from where she stood. Then quarterback
Mark Sanchez arrived; he took up the slack
And handled her like a pro. She played the hand
She had been dealt, but swore she'd never crawl.

CURRENCY: A SONNENIZIO

"The marvelous current of forgotten things," William Wordsworth,
Artegal and Elidure.

The marvelous current of forgotten things
Drains down Styx till it is no longer current.
We remember a currant or a raisin,
Currently, of our former youthful love life:
Half-baked, doughy, a largely fruitless courante
Danced upon the car seat of a jalopy.
Yes, of course, we wished it to last forever—
Or a thousand years at least of intercourse.
Our first lass, alas! is precursor only,
Never a courtesan for eternities.
Therefore currently we try to remember
What once the world was like riding that current
Now that we've wasted all of youth's currencies
And such occasions are non-occurrences.

VENUS' ARBOR

Hour on hour I've wandered Venus' arbor
Looking for the sun. All I encounter
Is dappled leaves and lichen. In her bower
She stands unarmed. Each time I try to mount her

I fall dismembered to the harlot moss,
The victim of her concrete passion, dazzled
And confused. I try to fit my loss
Into her cross words, but my mind is puzzled—

Incomplete and wretched intellect
Is no help at all. Before the tomb
Of love I stand and pray to be elect,
To be at one with her in her blue womb,

For there at least and last I could not fault her,
And I'd have no more reason to assault her.

SONNETS OF GOLD
For Jean—*June 16, 1956—2006 & 2011*

I.

Half a century has passed beyond
The pale of years since you walked down the aisle
To join me where my pastoral father waited
To preach at us before he tied the knot.
We stood there at attention to hear The Word
As I had done each Sunday all my life—
Now, one last time, and you became my wife.
I can't remember anything I heard
While we stood there; I don't remember what,
If anything, I thought. My father, sated
At last, gave us his blessing and our trial
Was over. We were able to abscond.

Alas, my dear, your trial had but begun.
Most likely it will end with a final pun.

II.

Five years more have passed us by since then
And we are at that pass again. A lass?—
You haven't been for half a century.
A lad? Aladdin has been bottled up in me
For just as long. No doubt it's far too crass
To mention things like this. Remember when
I couldn't say "remember when" because
There was no "then" and hardly any "was"?

Well, here we are, still idling—at least we're running,
And we may make it for another year
Of doing this and that . . . a bit of this,
Bestowing now and then an evening kiss
And then a dab of that. Alas! I fear
I see you've turned your ears off to my punning.

Seasoning

SEASONING

Yellow bird—the yellow bird is lying
Along the wind and under the green tree.
The cherry blooms blossom upon the tree
While the springtime wind arises flying.

Black bird—the black bird has taken to its wing
Along the wind, beside the singing tree.
The blossoms are dropping beneath the bright tree,
While the summer wind goes breathing, whispering.

Red bird—the red bird's wings, aflame, go burning
Along the wind, flaring from tree to tree.
The snow drops rattling through the bare tree;
The autumn wind among the leaves is turning.

I hear the night hawk—the night hawk's voice is calling—
The wind is rising as the night and leaves come falling.

A LETTER FROM LONDON
October 1993

Nothing is to be heard in the room except
The traffic of night moving on Doughty Street.
I have been spending time when I should have slept
Engaging my mind in acts of self-deceit.

What am I doing here alone in London?
If only I had come when I was young.
I've spent a fortnight getting nothing done,
Gathering notes for music that won't be sung.

I feel the city is a vast museum,
Not running with juices like a roast of beef,
But gelid fish and chips—a mausoleum
Built to inter the relics of one's belief.

I'm sorry to sound so damnably dark and dour.
Ambition burns feebly in the eleventh hour.

THANKSGIVING SONNET

The turkey's found its silence. So have we,
The young ones and the elders of the hall
Who welcomed back both staid and prodigal
With equal eyes. Each knows his own degree

Of happiness on any other day
But this when neural tides must flood or fall
To reach the level commonest to all
And flagrant colors fade to neutral gray.

This room's a simple basin of the sea
We yearly swim. Here lies the quiet bay
Where no one claims the single right of way,
Where each is bound to set the other free.

The beaches of this cordial shore forestall
The breakers dimly heard beyond the wall.

WINTER BLINDS

The winter evening lies beyond my blinds
Waiting for me to listen to its lies.
Why should I do so? It merely falsifies
The bitter wind whining at what it finds
Lying behind my glass. It takes all kinds
Of dusks to make November. The evening tries
To scratch the pane with air, with the stuff of sighs—
A skein of tales and yarns, but it unwinds

And lies there breathing hard. How can one live
To tell the truth? Lie in the night with eyes
And ears wide open, hearing the pantomime,
Or seeing the shadow world, of passing time?
To do so may be daring but not wise.
Best wind a skein of rime about the fictive.

CURSORY COMMENT

Summer follows spring and winter, fall.
Yes, summer follows spring and winters fall
Swift as a river one cannot dam at all.

In spring we hear the robin sing and call,
Autumn brings the bob-white's whistling call—
The owl in winter screeches to appall.

Summer's flood of birdsong must enthrall
Everyone with its power to enthrall
Swift as a river one cannot dam at all,

But which of us would not wish to forestall
The sounds of winter? Would we not forestall
The owl in winter screeching to appall?

The owl in winter screeches to appall,
For wintertime is winter, damn it all!

THE XMAS BLUES

It's Christmas Eve down at the Cabaret.
The combo's swinging at the Cabaret—
Some of the dancers are in disarray.

We're waiting for Santa to come jiving by,
Jiving along as he comes juking by,
ringing his bells and flying kind of high.

Jerry whacks the keys, George bops the vibes,
Hugh hoots his horn while George raps on the vibes
And here and there a customer imbibes

A cup of nog or a glass of scuppernong,
A mug of yuletide cheer or some scuppernong
To help him listen to the Turk's torchsong.

The band is wailing and Santa's overdue.
He's sporting red, but he'll be swinging blue.

TYRANNY

It's February now, and it is snowing.
It started snowing back in bleak November
And kept on snowing all through cold December.
But that was nothing. In January flowing
Snow came riding bareback on the blowing
Wild west wind. No one could remember
A colder month or a more arctic winter.
It's still that way. If anything, it's growing

Worse and worse. We're halfway through the month,
And nothing's getting better. We are still
Buried in the deep-freeze—crème-de-menthe
On ice-cream. Borealis, it takes some skill
To be a tyrant. Call yourself a mensch?
This isn't cruelty, it's overkill.

THE MILD WINTER BLUES

Where are those snows, those snows of yesteryear?
I mean, where have they gone, those yesteryear
Snows we used to plow through? They're not here,

And that's for sure. The January wind
Is hardly wind at all—a late March wind
At worst. What did they do, go and rescind

Winter? What is this, a "greenhouse" easing,
An ozone-acid-rainfall-smoggy easing
Into June forever? Alaska's freezing!

It's eighty below zero up in Barrow!
Nothing works in Barrow that you can borrow,
Beg or steal, not even people. Tomorrow?

Much the same, they say, or worse. Oh, whether
It changes or not, the weather is the weather.

WINTER PANES

Wings are fretting across my winter panes.
A downy hammers on his square of suet.
A nuthatch and her partner do a duet
Or flickering duel in which neither gains
Or loses much. Now, as the season wanes
An owl asks none too wisely, "Sir, to wit:
To whom may I be hooting?" "You may rue it
To find that out," I say, but he explains

By asking that same question one more time.
I shake my head and argue it no further
But watch the seeds receding in my feeder.
A chickadee asks me if I will feed her
Once more before it's dark. She shakes a feather
To ask me not to turn again to rhyme.

YEARSEND
A Carol Sonnet

This year is almost at its bitter end;
The year is coming to its bitter end
Just beyond the midnight's darkest bend.

It's over with—there's no use to pretend
It's not. It's over, no use to pretend
The year impending will not soon descend

And fall on us, for Chronus will upend
The next four seasons. We will surely spend
Them all beyond this darkest midnight's bend.

We should be watchful, clear-eyed, not pretend—
Put on an act attempting to pretend
The year impending will not soon descend;

Our looming seasons clearly must descend.
To fall upon us past this midnight's bend.

Simulacra

SHALL I COMPARE THEE TO A WINTER'S DAY?

Shall I compare thee to a winter's day?
Thou art more frigid and less temperate.
Rough winds do shake the windows where I stay
Alone in bed with no hope of a date.
The eye of heaven blinks and seldom shines,
His golden visage is forever dimmed.
Life is unfair and swiftly it declines.
The Yuletide yew we hewed remains untrimmed—
It will be sere by April, it will fade
As though it had been drying in an oast.
Death brags that thou art fondest of his shade
As is a well-known fact from coast to coast.
    So long as I may breathe or my eyes see,
    I'll rue the cold day I lay next to thee.

SIMULACRUM SONNET

Mohammed's Heaven has no extra virgin
Just for you, there is no manioc
To feed those men who are anonymous,
Engaged in ventures that are Picaresque,
Like searching for another Semele,
To maybe loot the dragon's hidden booty
Or possibly find the treasure-hoard of Lisbon.
More likely you would find a Lesbian
Awaiting you, one that was no beauty,
Either, whose figure was a simile
Hardly to be considered picturesque,
Unlike the burning bush euonymus
That colors autumn like a maniac
Risen to stress New England's extroversion.

THE OIL SPILL BLUES

The captain caught a thirst and left the helm.
He said, "Third mate, come here and take the helm,
I'm going to go below and overwhelm

A fifth of Scotch." The mate gave him relief.
He had no papers, but it was his belief
That he was smart enough to miss a reef

Marked on every map as black as ink,
As large as life and just as black as ink.
But, no, he wasn't. At least they didn't sink.

And now there's miles of slick on everything—
The otter's fur, the rocks—on everything
Alive or dead, afloat or on the wing.

The ship is on the reef. It's underhelmed.
The captain feels no pain. He's underwhelmed.

LISBON

Your ribbed green landscape frowns above its granite
Irises, and stony pupils stare
Out upon the turmoil of their planet.

Lisbon, one can see your mossy glances
Stumbling down an antique marble stair;
One can hear you whisper your romances—

Bright doubloons and noble wooden ships,
Canvas spread to seize the wind and sun,
Cavaliers intent on midnight lips . . . ,

But these are gone now and the world is new.
The past has slipped its knot and is undone,
Adrift upon the main without a clew.

Listen for a moment to your tutor:
Read the news. Go purchase a computer.

GIRLGUY

One-half of me makes love to the other half,
Yes, half of me makes love to the other half—
Being born hermaphroditic was a gaffe.

My first half feels so good when it makes love,
Oh, so awful good when it makes love,
My other half loves when push comes to shove.

One-half of me is Sicilian: ah! amore!
Take time to make a little love some more, eh?
I love to jump my bones in a little foray!

The other half is Dane and Brit . . . it's bolder,
Made of rocks and grit, a little boulder:
It's getting softer as I'm growing older.

One can't have everything that's on the shelf . . . .
I thank my lucky stars I have myself.

THE BLUES BLUES

I'm sitting singing sad songs by the ton,
Yes, sitting singing sad songs by the ton
And using up my stock of alliteration.

I love to hear the sibillant syllables dance,
The sibillant syllables slide around and dance,
But maybe I should start using consonance.

I'm using light rhymes now in each line three,
But no consonance so far. Three by three
The lines grow thick and quickly, ace, deuce, trey—

There! There's a consonance! A nimble one,
If I say so myself, a nimble one,
Though in line two there's extra repetition,

But them's the blues—they live on saying twice
When once would be enough and should suffice.

CATACHRESIS

At times I feel that I'm a *cloud in trousers*,
A pair of Dutchman's breeches casting shadows
Across the sun as I scuff through the meadows
Of afternoon over the heads of dowsers

Seeking fountains while they wait for showers
To fall from heaven and renew the credos
They've forsworn. They go on scribing dados
On the altars where once they were espousers

But now are merely alterers. We ignorers
Of such turnabouts seek out rodeos
Peopled by stars who tune their celestial radios
To the clown baiting the bull that glowers

At the spangled and bravely dressed toreros
Who stand, swords drawn, awaiting a storm of sorrows.

THE WORMY BLUES

I feel the worm again down in my craw,
That worm the harpy Fate stuffed down my craw
While I stood staring with a gaping maw.

I shut my mouth, but it was far too late.
I shut it slowly and a lot too late—
I had to swallow down the worm of Fate.

My gullet is its home. It wiggles there.
It's found itself a home—it likes it there!
It makes me choke and retch till I could swear . . . ,

Except my new pet worm gets in the way.
The words can't slide on by—it's in the way
Of everything I try to do or say,

So I will write it out, make my pet worm
Writhe upon the page, wriggle and squirm.

THE WANNABE BLUES
A Dramatic Monologue

I've published twenty "poems," maybe less,
In twenty years of teaching, more or less . . . ,
I wouldn't know my arsis from a stress.

The trouble is, my workshop students do!
I teach what little I know, oh, yes I do,
But what they know is making me feel blue.

They know how Shakespeare writes, how Milton can,
And Wordsworth, Chaucer, Poe—my students can
Sit down and read a poem and hear it scan!

I write "free" verse, but I am up a tree,
Out on a limb of that proverbial tree
When it comes to a consideration of rhythm and of the Nature
                                                    of Poetry.

I'd best let students teach my class, I sense;
I've not been issued my poetic license.

THE BLUE FLAG

Bluer than the bluest blue of sky,
The flag of friendship ripples overhead,
But when that flag is struck, friendship is dead
And enmity ensues: no flag can fly

That changes color in mid-flight. The sun
Will bleach a banner to a shade of white
When loyalty begins to bleed. Midnight
Descends, and dawn shows colors that have run

In broken trust that cannot be re-dyed.
The cloth hangs from its pole in rags and tatters,
For what it stood for once no longer matters.
Friendship survives and thrives in mutual pride:

The maxim must apply to everyone,
For when the flag is struck, what's done is done.

ASSUMPTIONS

Benny Hill said never to assume,
Never, never, never to assume
Anything at all, avoid the doom

That follows when you think you know it all,
When there is nothing you don't know at all,
Or so you think—you think that there is small

Chance that you'll be wrong, that you are wise
Beyond all others, for you've been a wise
Guy all your life and can't be otherwise

Than a prophet and a seer, a mage,
A major magus on a pilgrimage
To know it all, a mastermind and sage

Smarter than Benny Hill who thought that he
Was a wiser ASS than U or ME.

Prufrock's Dream

DREAMING STORIES

"I'd rather you avoid nightmares—though your fiction is welcome."
Miriam Kotzin, Editor, Per Contra.

I like to feed my nightmares hawthorn straw
That makes their motile lips writhe in disdain
And bridle at the thought of eating claw-

Mottled strands of vine that cause them pain.
They then become steeds of another color
That strain to taint my dreams with the vivid stain

Of sanguinary mood and bloody horror
That give me leave to delve into the dark
Niches and corners of death's corridor

Where wolfhounds howl and flying foxes bark
Along the fictive trail that leads to where
My story wakes and is willing to embark

Upon the ship of words that conjures awe
And makes the thudding heart stick in one's craw.

THE BORN-AGAIN BLUETH

For John Knapp, author of the book of religious children's poems, A Pillar of Pepper.

O Lord, forgive him! he knoweth not what he doth.
Forgive poor John! He knoweth not what he doth,
Nor what he ith, shall be, or what he wath.

When in his youth he thought for lore and warmth,
When he required withdom, Lord, and warmth,
Hith teacher handed John *The Book of Formth*.

John devoured it; now he but nibbleth
At Mother Goothe, Lord! merely nibbleth,
Hunting The Word, yet finding only "shibboleth."

A thouthand prayerth John raitheth to the thkieth --
Orithonth in cloudth thent to the thkieth
With many tearth and many thoulful thighth.

Back to *The Book*, John, the good *Book* of thy Youth!
Try to revivify thy early Muthe.

THE OXYMORONIC BLUES

I got a letter from my old friend John,
A funny letter from my poet-pal John—
He wants an example of an oxymoron!

"What is it?" he asks, "A phrasal self-destructor?
A trope, a figure of speech that will self-destruct or
cause an embolism in an instructor?"

I'm as surprised as a sloppily neutered bull,
as a particularly stupid neutered bull
sheepish because he's suddenly had the wool

pulled over his eyes. My head begins to whirl,
my eyes begin to swivel in a heady whirl
as I try to think . . . to think about a girl

in such a pinch, a woman whose round eyes
make a *silent commotion* of surprise.

THE DEPARTMENT MEETING BLUES

I've got the old Department Meeting blues.
I'm sitting in a meeting with the blues.
That's all I do—I'm always paying dues

And getting nowhere, nothing for my pains.
I'm feeling all my years-in-harness pains:
"No pain, no gain!" they say. There are no gains,

Just two steps back for every backward step—
A stumble here, a trip-up there, a step
In quicksand or, at best, an awkward schlep.

Now Blank is talking. How Blank loves to talk!
And talk and talk and talk and talk and talk.
Another word and I get up and walk.

It's 5:15! Get set; okay, here goes—
I'm shuffling paper . . . leaning . . . on my toes . . . .

WHEN DID I LOVE THEE?

When did I love thee? Let me count the days:
First, there was Sunday in a boozy haze.
I woke on Monday with an aching head
And couldn't get up, so I stayed in bed.
Tuesday came, I lost it on the fly;
Thought about it Wednesday . . . didn't try.
Then on Thursday I had so much to do
To make up for those weekdays that I blew
That Friday caught me napping unawares.
I tried to rise—I made it to the stairs

And fell asleep and down. I broke my leg.
Now Saturday's arrived. I'm drunk again.
Tomorrow when I wake I guess I'll beg
Forgiveness till I've no idea when.

EPISTLE IN DEPRESSION

For H. R. C., Jr., who sent an anonymous letter complaining that his anonymously submitted poem had been judged unfairly in a contest, 14 March 2009.

I'm not to blame that you are "bent and broke"
(Not to mention bankruptured and broken)
Because you spent your savings—every token,
Apparently, in your retirement poke—

Upon self-publication and ego trips
Foreign and domestic. Nor did I worsen
Your situation purposely, or coarsen
Your talents by applying contest judgeships

To work which you submitted that failed to win.
Those contests were anonymous, please note;
So, too, was the epistle that you wrote
Implying that *your* losses were *my* sin.

I doubt it, dear old friend, but I do worry
That you are in distress, and I am sorry.

PRUFROCK'S DREAM

The lower half of a mermaid's problematic:
How does one get to her through all those scales?
I've wondered from Woods Hole to the Adriatic,
I've examined dugongs and various types of whales,

But nothing seems to help me solve this mess,
Though I've considered everything from the rape
Of their golden locks to ravishing Loch Ness.
I swim quite well—I've stroked around the Cape

Of Good Hope a dozen times at dawn,
Mentally at least. I hear the maids
Singing in my dreams. I fear they're drawn
To others of their kind, to breasts and braids . . . .

"I hear the mermaids singing each to each"
As I swim after them from beach to beach.

PRUFROCK IN A NUTSHELL
And in anagram rhyme

Sometimes you need to hope for something large
To happen—you hope and pray for something large.
You need a blast, something with boom and glare!

Even though it's spring it seems like winter.
It may be mild, but still it seems like winter—
Your quilt is not a comfort but a twiner

That muffles you in dreams you can't recall,
In dreams you know you'd rather not recall
Like that abusive message from the midnight caller.

You need just once to be a major mage,
A Magus Magister, no minor mage—
You need to belt the run that wins the game!

You want to hear the shout and not the whimper
Fate likes to hand to you perhaps perwhim.

BLOOMSDAY

Today the prodigal returns once more
To roam the cobbled streets of Dublin town,
Returns to raise a toast, to blow the foam
From the glass of his ancestral home,
To quaff its best and take its lifeblood down
Where it will do some good. He will ignore
The little minds, the folk who drove him out
When he was nothing more than a youngling lout,

For now he is their hero, nothing less,
And they will celebrate again this day
The fellow with a pen who, in distress,
Left Ireland to wend an exile's way
Until he could see clear the winding track
That he might take to find the true way back.

A MIDSUMMER NIGHT'S PARTSONG
A terza-anagram-rima sonnet

I once upon a time could bend an elbow
With any fellow. I very seldom refused
To take or bestow a round. I've lain below

Many a friendly table till morning freed us
And we were able to forsake the nomad lees
Of empty soldiers. But time is a defuser,

And all that are left to us now are lemonades—
No longer may we debauch with Oberon
And quaff the flagons containing his demon ales

Of which he was the liberal midnight booner.
We never said we'd had enough, refused
His offer for fear that he would not reboon.

Our partsong has become a used etude
And fades at dusk now into desuetude.

The Unremembered

THE JOURNEY

The world is too much with us. Sooner or later
We have to let it go, and when we do
Who knows where it will go? We'll need a greater
Place to inhabit—perhaps a dead volcano
On Antares or a spinning top
In a sandstorm that cannot stand to stop
Blowing dusty souls to Hell and back.
Somehow we need to get our lives on track

Again. Or do we? Let the damn thing go.
We've been alive as long as necessary
To get a few things done, be young and grow
Old enough to drop what we've had to carry
Over the River of Time against its flow
Into the wilderness of the endless prairie.

THE BARN OWL

We strolled in the full flood of the moon that night
The barn owl woke, arose, flew out of sight.
Fate is but a sleight of the moon by night—

We stood as still as the mouse within its lair
Filling its lungs with the liquid summer air,
Listening for wing beats outside its lair

Where the barn owl rose into the oak
And gazed down into the limpid night like smoke
Coiling about the bole of the living oak.

We stood there with the smoky scent of the dark
Curling out of the shaggy oak tree's bark,
We stood and listened in the silent dark—

The timid mouse in its lair was out of sight—
Or so it felt in the roots of the twining night.

KNELL FOR JOHN KNELL
May 26, 2015

Last night I dreamed about my nephew John
For whom the tolling chimes forever knell.
We both were young as before the shadow fell,
Fell across his mind and then upon
This unperfected world that from then on
In imperfection was required to dwell.
The mourning songs of the steeple rise and swell,
Then settle with the shadows on the lawn.

He was, in fact, no nephew but my son
Before I had a son. I told him tales
And sang him songs when he was very small
And sat among his several cousins, all
About an age: the image never fails,
Not even when I wake and dreams are gone.

YOUNGER IN OUR DREAMS

We're always younger in our dreams. Old age
Sleeps in a trundle under the ancient bed
Waiting for daylight to tremble through the pane
And draw us out of shadow into rage
Once again. Why have we lived in vain
So long? We should have joined the silent dead
In their enjoyment of a joyless sleep.

Why do we kiss the surface? Embrace the deep
Where many other fugitives have fled
To avoid the pain of living. We dream again
That we are young and not the ancient sage
We thought we were, awake. We seem to strain
Against the draw of darkness. Let's live instead
Where there are wars and loves that we may wage.

HELLO AND GOODBYE

Thank you, John, for coming to say hello
Last night—you never said farewell,
But who could have the foresight to foretell
The bloody brainstorm that felled you with a blow?

You thought it was your mother who would go
Before too long; therefore, while she was well,
You went to visit her before she fell
Victim to age. The Laughing God is so

Perverse! He is sardonic, as we know.
He sits upon Cloud Ten, emits a smell
That makes us gag, reminding us of Hell
And that He cannot bear the status quo.

You left too soon and left us wondering why.
Thank you, John, for coming to say goodbye.

ELEGIAC SONNET
For Roger D.-B.

Thank you, Roger, for recollecting me
While you were dying, and asking Catherine,
Your daughter, to send your last two books along
When you were gone. Thank you for your song
Steeped as it is in the Muse's wine.
I witness you in your final agony

Remembering our friendship, and I will bring
Your image to my mind to say farewell
As best I may in the distances of time
And space that sunder us. I'll say in rime
What I can say by heart; I shall not dwell
On separations, for I would rather sing

Of a fellowship dependent on no man's mart,
But a friendship made and spent in language art.

THE UNREMEMBERED

I hear ethereal whispers, persuasive, soft and still,
"Daughter, if you don't remember us, who will?" – Author unknown.

We are your folk who slid away one night
Into the spiral shadows of the cave.
We hope that you have not forgotten us
As we, alas! have not remembered you—
The Lethal river winds arose and blew
Our minds away, if we had any focus
Left before life ended. Now the wave
Of time has torn us from revealing light.

None will remember us, of course, nor should
The living keep the brooding dead alive,
Although the very atoms of our flesh
Have been reused a billion times afresh
And nothing can recall us or revive
Except the double helix of our blood.

COSMOLOGY

The scientists say that what is going on
Is still the Bang that first emerged from nothing,
Becoming shortly everything that's known.
Not *all*, however, for a little something

Must have been left over: our balloon
Swells with altitude in the summer air,
Seeming to grow larger, like the moon
Sailing though an evening soft and fair.

But what about our bursting universe?
What is the "air" in which it must expand?
Since "outer space" is, though it seems perverse,
Part of the cosmos, is something else more grand

Surrounding us? Something we must face
Beyond Creation? Outer-outer space?

Coronations

THE CROWN OF BLUES
A dramatic monologue

My boss pulled off the worst of his mean acts—
He handed me the glare, and then the axe.
That was the situation, those are the facts.

What had I done to make him use an adze?
All I had done was manufacture ads.
Okay, so maybe I had used some pads—

They were too long, filled with a little air.
He could have chewed me out, said not to err.
I would have stopped. Now I sit here and wear

A hair-shirt made of my remaining hair.
I should have said to him, "Jawohl, mein herr!
But what you're doing simply isn't fair!"

But I said nothing. Now I guess that I'll
Just sit here brooding on my desert isle.

I sit here brooding on my desert isle—
Not since my bride and I walked down the aisle
Have I been out of work. It's been a while

Since she and I stood there before the altar,
A good long while since I have had to alter
The way I live. I'm too damn old to falter,

And I can't even say these things aloud.
I can't express my fears. It's not allowed
Among my friends and peers . . . the ad-game crowd,

The baby-boomers. No one would be awed
By such behavior. We'd just think it odd.
We'd shake our heads and mutter, "Oh, my God!"

And look away. Not one of us would waffle.
No skin off our nose! We'd treat the fellow awful.

No skin off our nose! We'd treat the fellow awful
Or worse. We'd look away, treat him like offal
Until he understood we'd had a crawful,

Just like the boss. We'd turn our eyes away
Until he heard the song, "Anchors Aweigh"
Ringing in his inner ear. We'd say,

"Tough luck, old boy," leave him holding the ball,
Standing there as though he'd start to bawl
Soon as we turned our backs. Our skin would crawl

And we would feel as though we couldn't bear
The thought of standing there like that as bare
As any new-born babe. We didn't dare

Think of ourselves in his shoes, our fists balled,
Eyes watering, getting pudgy, going bald.

Eyes watering, getting pudgy, going bald,
I waited till I got home, then I bawled
In the bathroom. Finally I hauled

My ass out to get me a little booze,
Confront my wife, and listen to her boos.
I didn't see what more I had to lose.

I soon found out. Not since the baby's birth
Had Susan given me a wider berth—
My sacking took away most of my worth;

That night in bed the rest of it just blew
Out the door. I lay there feeling blue
Or worse—self-pitying, and that sense grew

Until I turned into a crushing bore
And saw myself as nothing but a boor.

I saw myself as nothing but a boor,
But Susan saw me as a rutting boar—
She almost shoved me off onto the floor.

Then one day I blew up, called her a whore,
A wrinkled crone, frosty, cold and hoar.
She said, "I cannot take you one day more!"

And kicked me out. I had some money cached,
I thought, until one day a check I cashed
Bounced higher than an old employee trashed.

So now I'm on the dole and down the chute
And I'm considering whom I should shoot,
My boss or me, or just go on a toot

And make it permanent. I ought to censor
Such remarks. I was a common-senser—

I used to be a normal common-senser,
But now I'm smokin' mad, a mad incenser
Half the time, the other half I'm tenser

Than a wire. I'm far too old to hire—
The ladder of ambition goes no higher.
But I am still too youthful to retire,

Or so they tell me. What's a guy to do,
Lie on the grass and wait until the dew
Falls on my face? I haven't got a clue.

My wife and kids are gone, the house as well . . . ,
If I could find one I'd jump down a well
And fall the last few feet on the road to Hell.

I wake up every morning to nothing new:
What's there to do? I only wish I knew.

What's there to do? I only wish I knew!
I feel like I'm the last remaining gnu
In what is left of the fabulous Bronx zoo.

Here I sit, existing like a friar
In a dark back room with a coffee pot and fryer
Remembering what things were like in a prior

Life someplace out there in the great World's Fair
Where people could afford their subway fare,
Clean sheets, a table and a comfy chair

Or sit at a desk where maybe they relax
A bit too much sometimes, are a little lax,
But still they don't get handed those dirty sacks—

I once was one of those commercial hacks.
My boss pulled off the worst of his mean acts.

A CROWN FOR DON
Donald Justice, August 12, 1925 - August 6, 2004

Dear Don,
         Of course we knew you'd have to leave;
We hoped not, but we saw you had to leave.
We understood there could be no reprieve.

We knew you young, we knew you when we all
Were young, with you included—when we all
Were tangled in the language, held in thrall

By sound and meter: couplet, quatrain, thrime,
By rhythm in the line, caesura, rhyme—
You were the boy who showed us how to chime.

You read our work with care, closely, with care.
You read us with intelligence and care.
You let your annoyance show, but you were fair.

Head among our clouds, you liked to prime
Rhymes with something like the mountain's tone.

Rhymes with something like the mountain's tone,
Stone echoing the sounds of emptiness
Nestling in the words that you interred,
Winter–like, in leaves you used to browse,

Brows creased in concentration; there, ahead,
Wedded to what looked like a granite head
Limned upon a tor by hoary rime,
Blown to a ledge where rams might snort and browse

Testily on sparseness, we would atone
Less for what you sprung than you implied.
Enter summer coasting past the ness:
Dead astern there lay the emptiness
Time left behind once you had gone ahead,
Gone past those frozen lines we now inter.

Gone past those frozen lines we now inter,
Destined never now to see their prime
And interlined with icy monotone,

We settled down into a musing winter
Incapable, we hoped, of petty crime
Or felonies to which we once were prone

Against the language. For years we made believe
That we were you. We stood before our classes
And taught the young as you were wont to do,

And then, while you still lived, we had to leave
All of those young men and lovely lasses
Ourselves and lie down in the fallen dew,

For we too had grown old, though it is true
We never could have overtaken you.

We never could have overtaken you,
Although we strove hard as we ever could.
We grew our holly, felled the silver yew,
Loaded the ingle, burned the sylvan wood.

We waited for the elves to load the sleigh.
We bode and hoped the gift would yet arrive
And fall onto our sheets. We could not slay
Desire for Erato. We would strive

To lure her to lie down upon our leaves
And murmur love duets. Sometimes she would,
No matter what the jealous world believes,
Sometimes that fickle goddess whom we wooed

Spent nights with us and left behind a token
Word that hitherto we'd left unspoken.

Word that hitherto we've left unspoken,
Make yourself manifest! Word of disease,
Word that makes us tremble, leaves us broken,
Word that fills its victims with unease,

Stand down, Parkinson's! Now let us stare
At your hateful syllables. You turn
A normal man into something rare:
An aspen made of flesh whose branches churn

Without a breeze to churn them. You make us shiver
As though the summertime had turned to winter.
The leaves we write upon begin to quiver
And the letters dance, begin to splinter

Into fragments of what we would write—
Our thoughts like frightened birds burst into flight.

Our thoughts like frightened birds burst into flight.
Ideas gutter, then they flicker out,
Shadows engorge the mind for lack of light,

The brain goes dry and in a state of drought
The wells of Helicon turn into dust.
The seed of inspiration cannot sprout,

The scent of attar is transformed to must
That fills the catacombs of Plato's cave.
No oil alleviates the film of rust

That snarls these lumbering joints. Each limb is slave
To whims of illness. We wish that we could find
A stylus that would help us to engrave

One last verse, or even a single word
That wouldn't act as though it were absurd,

That wouldn't act as though it were a bird
Hanging upside-down upon a twig
Beneath which broods a very sorry bard
With droppings in his hair, taking a swig

Of elixir in a halt and clumsy manner.
Where is his lunch? Where is that moldy cheese
He brought with him because he'd lost his manna?
Where is that loaf that he would slice and grease

To succor him in this his sorry state
Of helplessness? And where is his inkwell
Filled with ichor of the gods? Too late,
It is too late to dip his gander quill

And write another line of how we grieve
For, Don, of course we knew you'd have to leave.

COUSIN JOSEPHINE
A Crown of Sonnets for Josephine Sardella Higgins,
Buffalo, New York, August 12, 2006

Dear cousin Jo, when I was but a tad
You baby-sat me when I wasn't good,
For which you knew the reason: You understood
Me better than my parents. As a lad
I joined the Navy just the way you had
During The War. Every time I could,
I visited you in your neighborhood
In San Diego. We were seldom sad—

That is, till now. We were the best of friends
All our lives, and we'll continue so
As long as I'm alive. I won't forget
How close we always were from the day we met,
But now we find that you are forced to go
Through that doorway where the future ends.

Through that doorway where the future ends
I see a lot of nothing standing by.
"Oh, Lewis," asked your uncle one day, "why
Must we grow old?" I guess it all depends
On what that inquiry of his portends,
For he was pushing sixty then, while I
Was in my teens. He said it with a sigh,
As I recall, and my reply impends

Now as then. I was amazed he'd ask
His replacement generation such a thing.
I stared at him. I had no answer, for
I'd never pondered it. It's still a task
To wrap my mind around such questioning.
"Because we do, that's all." There's nothing more.

"Because there's nothing more," I should have said,
Perhaps, but he was a religious man,
A minister no less. If I began
To doubt while I was young, still I would dread
To tell him so. I stalled a bit instead
Of saying, "I won't be a clergyman.
I can't believe that silly stuff." I ran
Away to sea when school was done. I fled

Instead of waiting for the coming fall
When classmates would be starting to attend
Their colleges. My folks were poor. It all
Seemed obvious to me, so why not blend
My fate with obligation? Why forestall
The doom that circumstance seemed to intend?

The doom that circumstance seemed to intend
Turned out to be an aircraft carrier,
Its predecessor a famous harrier
Of World War II, the *Hornet*. I would spend
Two years before her mast, and we would wend
Our way around the world: The barrier
To short cuts?—her derriére
Too large for the Panama, so they would send

Us through Suez instead. That's where we'd sail
After our shakedown in the Caribbean.
In the Red Sea I looked beneath the rail
And wondered what it was that I was seeing—
There lay beside us a shark large as a whale
Near the ocean's surface, a monstrous being.

Near the ocean's surface, a monstrous being
From the deep swam beside us keeping
The *Hornet* company. The desert's sweeping
Sands flew away to the horizons fleeing
Before the sun and evening shadows slipping
Out of the pyramids. The shark lay sleeping
Gray and motionless, yet somehow tipping
Balances about us, no two agreeing

On equipoise, the heavy heavens lying
Upon the desert threatening to glide
From underneath the ebbing, slowly dying
Day into night like the promised bride
Of the pharaoh silence breathing the heavy musk
Of the sarcophagus in the coming dusk.

Of the sarcophagus in the coming dusk
We never were to speak, for we had days
Yet to pursue, we had the numerous ways
Of fate to find before we felt the brusque
Dismissal of the grave. The narwhal's tusk
Could be avoided. There were subtle grays
And shades of darkness to endure, the plays
Of minnows and anchovies dodging cusk.

I lived through a typhoon in mid-Pacific,
Played on Oahu's beaches for a bit,
Sailed underneath the Golden Gate—terrific
Feat of engineering, that! We hit
The light fantastic and the sweet sublime.
Then we enjoyed our San Diego time.

Then we enjoyed our San Diego time
Together. You made pasta meals for me
And my shipmates. We attended the ballet
To see Maria Tallchief. The coastal clime
Was perfect for a while. I learned to rhyme
Better, began to publish poetry—
I did not know that that was soon to be
The way my life would go. And so our prime

Fell upon us and soon let us go
To take the wind away. It wasn't bad
For me, but Dad and Mom, your brother Joe,
And his wife Josie too—they all had
This plot for you here in Buffalo,
Dear cousin Jo, like when I was a tad.

AN OLD POET'S REPLY
To Keats' "When I Have Fears."

I have no fears that I may cease to be
Because my pen has gleaned my teeming brain,
Producing high-piled books—how many a tree
Has gone to make this pile? It's been a drain
On Nature. Did I join the human race
Willingly? I was not asked to dance,
To join this moiling throng whose flailings trace
Their fleeting shadows on the face of chance.

When I was young, fair creature of an hour,
I thought my sands would not too likely pour
Through my glass longer than they did through your
Narrow throat. But time will soon devour
My work as well—it causes me no grief.
Far from it; it will be a great relief.

Acknowledgments

"Blue Flag" first appeared on-line in *Autumn Sky Poems* DAILY on July 7th 2015; "The Oxymoronic Blues" first appeared in *Blue Unicorn*; "Catachresis" and "The Xmas Blues" in *The Café Review*; "A Letter from London" in *The Formalist*; "A Crown for Don" in *Measure*; "Catachresis," "Cosmology," "Cousin Josephine," "The Crown of Blues," "The Department Meeting Blues," "Embrace," and "Winter Panes" in *Per Contra*; "Prufrock in a Nutshell," "Sonnets of Gold," "Tyranny," and "Yearsend" in *The Tower Journal*; "Body Part" and "A Midsummer Night's Partsong" in Trinacria"; "Nocturne" in Sonnetto Poesia (Canada), and "Cursory Comment" in *Via*.

"The Oil Spill Blues" was published originally in *80 on the 80's*, ed. Robert McGovern and Joan Baranow, Ashland: Ashland Poetry Press, 1990.

"Venal Sonnets" ("Leola" and "Selene") were published originally in *Maine Taproot, An Anthology of Verse*, ed. Margaret Rockwell Finch *et alii*, Farmington, ME: Encircle Publications, 2010.

"Sports Sexual Harassment Embarrassment" and "Venus' Arbor" were published originally in *Hot Sonnets*, ed. Moira Egan and Clarinda Harriss, Washington, D C: Entasis Press, 2011.

About the Author

Lewis Turco was the founder of what are now the Cleveland State University Poetry Center and the Creative Writing Department of SUNY Oswego. He is the author of "the poets' Bible"—THE BOOK OF FORMS: A HANDBOOK OF POETICS (University Press of New England, 2012), in print for half a century in four editions since 1968 and of more than fifty other books, chapbooks, and monographs including A BOOK OF FEARS, winner, with translator Joseph Alessia, of the first annual Bordighera Bi-Lingual Poetry Prize (1998); VISIONS AND REVISIONS OF AMERICAN POETRY, winner of the Melville Cane Award for criticism of the Poetry Society of America (University of Arkansas Press, 1986), and of SATAN'S SCOURGE: A NARRATIVE OF THE AGE OF WITCHCRAFT IN ENGLAND AND NEW ENGLAND 1580-1697 (Star Cloud Press), winner of the Wild Card Category of the 2009 New England Book Festival. He has a B.A. from UConn and an M.A. from Iowa; since his retirement from teaching in 1996 he has received honorary doctorates from three institutions of higher education in Maine and Ohio.

VIA Folios

A refereed book series dedicated to the culture of Italians and Italian Americans.

JOE AMATO. *Samuel Taylor's Hollywood Adventure*. Vol. 129. Novel.
BEA TUSIANI. *con amore*. Vol. 128. Memoir.
MARIA GIURA. *What My Father Taught Me*. Vol. 127. Poetry.
STANISLAO PUGLIESE. *A Century of Sinatra*. Vol. 126. Popular Culture. $12
TONY ARDIZZONE. *The Arab's Ox*. Vol. 125. Novel. $18
PHYLLIS CAPELLO. *Packs Small Plays Big*. Vol. 124. Poetry.
FRED GARDAPHÉ. *Read 'em and Reap*. Vol. 123. Criticism. $22
JOSEPH A. AMATO. *Diagnostics*. Vol 122. Literature. $12.
DENNIS BARONE. *Second Thoughts*. Vol 121. Poetry. $10
OLIVIA K. CERRONE. *The Hunger Saint*. Vol 120. Novella. $12
GARIBLADI M. LAPOLLA. *Miss Rollins in Love*. Vol 119. Novel. $24
JOSEPH TUSIANI. *A Clarion Call*. Vol 118. Poetry. $16
JOSEPH A. AMATO. *My Three Sicilies*. Vol 117. Poetry & Prose. $17
MARGHERITA COSTA. *Voice of a Virtuosa and Coutesan*. Vol 116. Poetry. $24
NICOLE SANTALUCIA. *Because I Did Not Die*. Vol 115. Poetry. $12
MARK CIABATTARI. *Preludes to History*. Vol 114. Poetry. $12
HELEN BAROLINI. *Visits*. Vol 113. Novel. $22
ERNESTO LIVORNI. *The Fathers' America*. Vol 112. Poetry. $14
MARIO B. MIGNONE. *The Story of My People*. Vol 111. Non-fiction. $17
GEORGE GUIDA. *The Sleeping Gulf*. Vol 110. Poetry. $14
JOEY NICOLETTI. *Reverse Graffiti*. Vol 109. Poetry. $14
GIOSE RIMANELLI. *Il mestiere del furbo*. Vol 108. Criticism. $20
LEWIS TURCO. *The Hero Enkidu*. Vol 107. Poetry. $14
AL TACCONELLI. *Perhaps Fly*. Vol 106. Poetry. $14
RACHEL GUIDO DEVRIES. *A Woman Unknown in Her Bones*. Vol 105. Poetry. $11
BERNARD BRUNO. *A Tear and a Tear in My Heart*. Vol 104. Non-fiction. $20
FELIX STEFANILE. *Songs of the Sparrow*. Vol 103. Poetry. $30
FRANK POLIZZI. *A New Life with Bianca*. Vol 102. Poetry. $10
GIL FAGIANI. *Stone Walls*. Vol 101. Poetry. $14
LOUISE DESALVO. *Casting Off*. Vol 100. Fiction. $22
MARY JO BONA. *I Stop Waiting for You*. Vol 99. Poetry. $12
RACHEL GUIDO DEVRIES. *Stati zitt, Josie*. Vol 98. Children's Literature. $8
GRACE CAVALIERI. *The Mandate of Heaven*. Vol 97. Poetry. $14
MARISA FRASCA. *Via incanto*. Vol 96. Poetry. $12
DOUGLAS GLADSTONE. *Carving a Niche for Himself*. Vol 95. History. $12
MARIA TERRONE. *Eye to Eye*. Vol 94. Poetry. $14
CONSTANCE SANCETTA. *Here in Cerchio*. Vol 93. Local History. $15

MARIA MAZZIOTTI GILLAN. *Ancestors' Song*. Vol 92. Poetry. $14

MICHAEL PARENTI. *Waiting for Yesterday: Pages from a Street Kid's Life*. Vol 90. Memoir. $15

ANNIE LANZILOTTO. *Schistsong*. Vol 89. Poetry. $15

EMANUEL DI PASQUALE. *Love Lines*. Vol 88. Poetry. $10

CAROSONE & LOGIUDICE. *Our Naked Lives*. Vol 87. Essays. $15

JAMES PERICONI. *Strangers in a Strange Land: A Survey of Italian-Language American Books*.Vol 86. Book History. $24

DANIELA GIOSEFFI. *Escaping La Vita Della Cucina*. Vol 85. Essays. $22

MARIA FAMÀ. *Mystics in the Family*. Vol 84. Poetry. $10

ROSSANA DEL ZIO. *From Bread and Tomatoes to Zuppa di Pesce "Ciambotto"*.Vol. 83. $15

LORENZO DELBOCA. *Polentoni*. Vol 82. Italian Studies. $15

SAMUEL GHELLI. *A Reference Grammar*. Vol 81. Italian Language. $36

ROSS TALARICO. *Sled Run*. Vol 80. Fiction. $15

FRED MISURELLA. *Only Sons*. Vol 79. Fiction. $14

FRANK LENTRICCHIA. *The Portable Lentricchia*. Vol 78. Fiction. $16

RICHARD VETERE. *The Other Colors in a Snow Storm*. Vol 77. Poetry. $10

GARIBALDI LAPOLLA. *Fire in the Flesh*. Vol 76 Fiction & Criticism. $25

GEORGE GUIDA. *The Pope Stories*. Vol 75 Prose. $15

ROBERT VISCUSI. *Ellis Island*. Vol 74. Poetry. $28

ELENA GIANINI BELOTTI. *The Bitter Taste of Strangers Bread*. Vol 73. Fiction. $24

PINO APRILE. *Terroni*. Vol 72. Italian Studies. $20

EMANUEL DI PASQUALE. *Harvest*. Vol 71. Poetry. $10

ROBERT ZWEIG. *Return to Naples*. Vol 70. Memoir. $16

AIROS & CAPPELLI. *Guido*. Vol 69. Italian/American Studies. $12

FRED GARDAPHÉ. *Moustache Pete is Dead! Long Live Moustache Pete!*. Vol 67. Literature/Oral History. $12

PAOLO RUFFILLI. *Dark Room/Camera oscura*. Vol 66. Poetry. $11

HELEN BAROLINI. *Crossing the Alps*. Vol 65. Fiction. $14

COSMO FERRARA. *Profiles of Italian Americans*. Vol 64. Italian Americana. $16

GIL FAGIANI. *Chianti in Connecticut*. Vol 63. Poetry. $10

BASSETTI & D'ACQUINO. *Italic Lessons*. Vol 62. Italian/American Studies. $10

CAVALIERI & PASCARELLI, Eds. *The Poet's Cookbook*. Vol 61. Poetry/Recipes. $12

EMANUEL DI PASQUALE. *Siciliana*. Vol 60. Poetry. $8

NATALIA COSTA, Ed. *Bufalini*. Vol 59. Poetry. $18.

RICHARD VETERE. *Baroque*. Vol 58. Fiction. $18.

LEWIS TURCO. *La Famiglia/The Family*. Vol 57. Memoir. $15

NICK JAMES MILETI. *The Unscrupulous*. Vol 56. Humanities. $20

BASSETTI. ACCOLLA. D'AQUINO. *Italici: An Encounter with Piero Bassetti*. Vol 55. Italian Studies. $8

GIOSE RIMANELLI. *The Three-legged One*. Vol 54. Fiction. $15

CHARLES KLOPP. *Bele Antiche Stòrie*. Vol 53. Criticism. $25

JOSEPH RICAPITO. *Second Wave*. Vol 52. Poetry. $12

GARY MORMINO. *Italians in Florida*. Vol 51. History. $15

GIANFRANCO ANGELUCCI. *Federico F*. Vol 50. Fiction. $15

ANTHONY VALERIO. *The Little Sailor*. Vol 49. Memoir. $9

ROSS TALARICO. *The Reptilian Interludes*. Vol 48. Poetry. $15

RACHEL GUIDO DE VRIES. *Teeny Tiny Tino's Fishing Story*. Vol 47. Children's Literature. $6

EMANUEL DI PASQUALE. *Writing Anew*. Vol 46. Poetry. $15

MARIA FAMÀ. *Looking For Cover*. Vol 45. Poetry. $12

ANTHONY VALERIO. *Toni Cade Bambara's One Sicilian Night*. Vol 44. Poetry. $10

EMANUEL CARNEVALI. *Furnished Rooms*. Vol 43. Poetry. $14

BRENT ADKINS. et al., Ed. *Shifting Borders. Negotiating Places*. Vol 42. Conference. $18

GEORGE GUIDA. *Low Italian*. Vol 41. Poetry. $11

GARDAPHÈ, GIORDANO, TAMBURRI. *Introducing Italian Americana*. Vol 40. Italian/American Studies. $10

DANIELA GIOSEFFI. *Blood Autumn/Autunno di sangue*. Vol 39. Poetry. $15/$25

FRED MISURELLA. *Lies to Live By*. Vol 38. Stories. $15

STEVEN BELLUSCIO. *Constructing a Bibliography*. Vol 37. Italian Americana. $15

ANTHONY JULIAN TAMBURRI, Ed. *Italian Cultural Studies 2002*. Vol 36. Essays. $18

BEA TUSIANI. *con amore*. Vol 35. Memoir. $19

FLAVIA BRIZIO-SKOV, Ed. *Reconstructing Societies in the Aftermath of War*. Vol 34. History. $30

TAMBURRI. et al., Eds. *Italian Cultural Studies 2001*. Vol 33. Essays. $18

ELIZABETH G. MESSINA, Ed. *In Our Own Voices*. Vol 32. Italian/American Studies. $25

STANISLAO G. PUGLIESE. *Desperate Inscriptions*. Vol 31. History. $12

HOSTERT & TAMBURRI, Eds. *Screening Ethnicity*. Vol 30. Italian/American Culture. $25

G. PARATI & B. LAWTON, Eds. *Italian Cultural Studies*. Vol 29. Essays. $18

HELEN BAROLINI. *More Italian Hours*. Vol 28. Fiction. $16

FRANCO NASI, Ed. *Intorno alla Via Emilia*. Vol 27. Culture. $16

ARTHUR L. CLEMENTS. *The Book of Madness & Love*. Vol 26. Poetry. $10

JOHN CASEY, et al. *Imagining Humanity*. Vol 25. Interdisciplinary Studies. $18

ROBERT LIMA. *Sardinia/Sardegna*. Vol 24. Poetry. $10

DANIELA GIOSEFFI. *Going On*. Vol 23. Poetry. $10

ROSS TALARICO. *The Journey Home*. Vol 22. Poetry. $12

EMANUEL DI PASQUALE. *The Silver Lake Love Poems*. Vol 21. Poetry. $7

JOSEPH TUSIANI. *Ethnicity*. Vol 20. Poetry. $12

JENNIFER LAGIER. *Second Class Citizen*. Vol 19. Poetry. $8

FELIX STEFANILE. *The Country of Absence*. Vol 18. Poetry. $9

PHILIP CANNISTRARO. *Blackshirts*. Vol 17. History. $12

LUIGI RUSTICHELLI, Ed. *Seminario sul racconto*. Vol 16. Narrative. $10

LEWIS TURCO. *Shaking the Family Tree*. Vol 15. Memoirs. $9

LUIGI RUSTICHELLI, Ed. *Seminario sulla drammaturgia*. Vol 14. Theater/ Essays. $10

FRED GARDAPHÈ. *Moustache Pete is Dead! Long Live Moustache Pete!*. Vol 13. Oral Literature. $10

JONE GAILLARD CORSI. *Il libretto d'autore. 1860–1930*. Vol 12. Criticism. $17

HELEN BAROLINI. *Chiaroscuro: Essays of Identity*. Vol 11. Essays. $15

PICARAZZI & FEINSTEIN, Eds. *An African Harlequin in Milan*. Vol 10. Theater/Essays. $15

JOSEPH RICAPITO. *Florentine Streets & Other Poems*. Vol 9. Poetry. $9

FRED MISURELLA. *Short Time*. Vol 8. Novella. $7

NED CONDINI. *Quartettsatz*. Vol 7. Poetry. $7

ANTHONY JULIAN TAMBURRI, Ed. *Fuori: Essays by Italian/American Lesbiansand Gays*. Vol 6. Essays. $10

ANTONIO GRAMSCI. P. Verdicchio. Trans. & Intro. *The Southern Question*. Vol 5.Social Criticism. $5

DANIELA GIOSEFFI. *Word Wounds & Water Flowers*. Vol 4. Poetry. $8

WILEY FEINSTEIN. *Humility's Deceit: Calvino Reading Ariosto Reading Calvino*. Vol 3. Criticism. $10

PAOLO A. GIORDANO, Ed. *Joseph Tusiani: Poet. Translator. Humanist*. Vol 2. Criticism. $25

ROBERT VISCUSI. *Oration Upon the Most Recent Death of Christopher Columbus*. Vol 1. Poetry.

www.ingramcontent.com/pod-product-compliance
Lightning Source LLC
Chambersburg PA
CBHW051734040426
42447CB00008B/1123